Biographies of famous people to
support the curriculum.

Julius
Caesar

by Emma Fischel
Illustrations by Lesley Bisseker

W
FRANKLIN WATTS
NEW YORK • LONDON • SYDNEY

First published in 1998 by
Franklin Watts
96 Leonard Street
London
EC2A 4XD

Franklin Watts Australia
14 Mars Road
Lane Cove
NSW 2066

ISBN: 0 7496 2894 4

A CIP catalogue record for this book
is available from the British Library.

Dewey Decimal Classification Number: 937

10 9 8 7 6 5 4 3 2

Series editor: Sarah Ridley
Series designer: Kirstie Billingham
Consultant: Dr Anne Millard

Printed in Great Britain

Julius Caesar

In the last two thousand years
there have been many great
leaders all over the world.
There have been great leaders
in wartime and great leaders
in peace.

Gaius Julius Caesar
100~44 bc

And one of the greatest of them
all was Julius Caesar.

Julius Caesar was born in a city called Rome. People in Rome spoke a language called Latin.

'Canem'

Now Rome is the capital city of the country named Italy. Even then, over two thousand years ago, it was a big city — and a powerful one.

As a child, Caesar would have learnt what it meant to be Roman.

A great empire stretching over many Lands!

The best and biggest army in the world!

Builders of the finest bridges and roads!

Caesar was lucky to be born a boy. In those days people didn't think girls were nearly as important.

He was even luckier to be born a patrician boy. Patricians were the most powerful people in Rome.

Ours is a noble family.

The sort of job people did then depended on their family. If you were from an important family, you could get important jobs.

Most patrician boys were taught at home – and lessons started early.

Caesar learnt all the usual things children learn today. He learnt other things too, like philosophy, Greek and public speaking.

Caesar knew that making good speeches would help him be successful when he grew up, so he practised hard.

Every Roman should be rich enough to eat flamingo with dates!

Caesar's uncle, Marius, was a general and a leader of the Senate, the place where Rome's noblemen came to discuss how Rome should be ruled.

Members of the Senate were called senators. Most of them came from the same noble families.

Marius wanted to let in some new men. This made him very unpopular with some senators. But the people loved him.
He let poor men into the army and gave them land as a reward.

Marius had a great enemy, a very important general called Sulla.

Marius and Sulla each wanted to be the most powerful person in Rome – and each of them had big armies.

While Caesar was growing up, there were terrible wars between them.

87 bc
86 bc
85 bc
84 bc
83 bc

In the end, Sulla won. "Kill my enemies without trial!" he ordered. Caesar knew he had to leave Rome for a while, or Sulla might kill him.

13

Three years later Sulla died. Caesar came back to Rome. He knew what to do now.

"Lots of different jobs in the army and politics!" he said. "That's the way to the top!"

Quaestor!

Aedile!

Praetor!

Pontifex Maximus!

And bit by bit, he started to make a name for himself.

The votes of the rich count for more than the votes of the poor. Is this fair?

He fought in several wars and won a medal for bravery. He was also a successful lawyer.

When Caesar was about twenty-
five he was captured by pirates.
They demanded a huge ransom
to release him.

Caesar wasn't afraid of them.
"One day I will execute you all!"
he said.

16

The pirates just laughed.
They didn't believe him –
they should have done, though.

When he was released he
captured them. Then he executed
every single one.

Caesar, like other powerful
Romans, worked hard on making
himself popular with the people.
He ran up lots of debts by
putting on free entertainments.

Romans liked watching fast and
fierce chariot races. Gladiator
battles were popular, too.
The men fought each other to
the death.

Caesar was steadily working his way to the top.

The two most important men in Rome didn't like each other much, or trust each other.

But they both trusted Caesar.

With such powerful friends,
things happened fast for Caesar.
He was made a consul.

Together we three are power!

Congratulations Consul!

Consuls were put in charge of the
whole army and government.
Now Caesar was one of the most
important people in Rome.

By now Caesar was forty. His year as consul was a busy one.

When it ended, Caesar was
given command of an army.
He was about to begin nearly
ten long years of fierce fighting.

Caesar was tough on his army, but fair. The soldiers loved him.

"He eats with us, marches with us, he's first into battle and he even pays us on time!" they said.

And while they rested, he worked on.

Caesar and his army were in a place called Gaul, now called France. It was a divided land, full of fierce and warlike tribes.

The Gauls were clever fighters. But so was Caesar.

Caesar made sure news of all his victories went back to Rome – and so did his important prisoners.

Caesar wanted to conquer Britain too. He went there twice but both times terrible storms wrecked a lot of his ships.

The first time he didn't stay long.

The second time he brought back a bigger army and had more success – but not nearly as much as he wanted.

Although that wasn't quite how they heard it back in Rome.

Things had changed in Rome while Caesar was away. Crassus had died and Pompey was jealous of Caesar's success.

Many people thought Caesar should be made consul again on his return. Some people didn't though, and they were the ones Pompey listened to.

Too much power for Caesar.

Caesar sent a friend to Rome to try to mend things.

It was no use.

Caesar camped on the banks of a river called the Rubicon. It divided Gaul from Italy, where Pompey was.

Caesar knew that if his army crossed the river without permission it would mean war with Pompey and Rome.

At last Caesar made up his mind.

"It is a huge and terrible thing
I am about to do," he said.
Then he crossed the river.

Many more soldiers joined
Caesar's army as he marched
towards Rome.

After nearly two years of fierce fighting Caesar won – but at a terrible price.

Pompey fled to Egypt. Caesar followed him. He wanted to pardon him ...

but he was too late.

Caesar stayed in Egypt for two more years. A bitter battle for power was going on there.

"The throne is rightfully Cleopatra's, seized by her brother Ptolemy!" Caesar said. He helped Cleopatra regain the throne.

They had a son too.

My little Caesar!

Some of Pompey's supporters tried to fight Caesar in north Africa. It took another year but he crushed them all in the end.

Caesar had conquered lots of new places in his battles. Now Rome ruled over huge amounts of land.

THIS time Caesar would be treated well on his return.

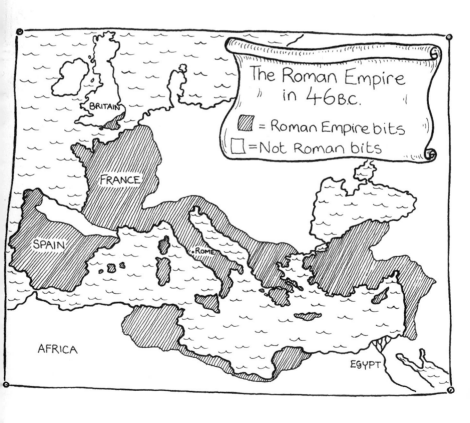

Caesar was made dictator, the absolute ruler of Rome. A few people had been made dictator before, but only for a short time. Julius was made dictator for life. Now no one could tell him what to do!

Caesar was now about fifty-five.
"To work!" he said. "I shall
bring order, peace and wealth
to Rome and all its lands."

But many rich and noble people were unhappy. "He thinks he is king! He stops us making so much money," they said.

They started to plot.
"The dictator must die!" they said. "But he must suspect nothing. His friends must strike at him first!"

His friends were hard to persuade but at last they agreed.

"Rome should not be governed by one man alone," they said sadly. "It is best we kill him."

The date was set. So was the place.

15th March.

Inside the Senate.

The day arrived. "Don't go to the Senate, Caesar," begged his wife, Calpurnia. "Something terrible will happen. I know from my dreams."

Still Caesar went.

"Read this at once, Caesar," pleaded a man on the way, handing Caesar a piece of paper. It warned Caesar about the plot to kill him.

But Caesar never got a chance to read it.

He stepped inside the Senate
and was stabbed to death.
He died of twenty-three wounds
at the foot of Pompey's statue.

Further facts

What happened next?

After Caesar was killed there was a big fight for power in Rome. In the end, his great-nephew Octavian won and became Emperor of Rome.

Caesar the writer

Caesar wrote a lot about his battles in Gaul. His writings tell us about how battles were fought in Roman times.

He described all the wild tribes he conquered too – and even the strange animals he found in the forests!

BC **and** AD

Time in history is divided into years BC and years AD. BC years are before Christ was born, AD years are after.

Caesar lived from 100BC to 44BC. BC stands for 'Before Christ', so 100BC means '100 years Before Christ'.

Some important dates in Julius Caesar's lifetime

100BC   Gaius Julius Caesar is born in Rome on 12 July.

76BC   Caesar captured by pirates in the Mediterranean.

60BC   Caesar teams up with Crassus and Pompey as leaders of Rome.

59BC   Caesar made consul for a year.

58BC   Battles in Gaul begin.

49BC   Caesar crosses the Rubicon River and starts a war with Pompey.

48BC   Caesar defeats Pompey at Pharsalus, Greece.

48BC   Caesar meets Cleopatra in Egypt and has a son.

46BC   Caesar returns to Rome and becomes dictator for life.

44BC   Caesar is murdered on 15 March.